The Mind of A Sociopath

Your Guide to Understanding The Anti-Social Personality Disorder Of Sociopaths

By
Michele Gilbert

Visit My Amazon Author Page

Dedicated to those who choose to stretch beyond their own limits and to seek a more abundant and fulfilling life

Your thoughts are creative.

Michele Gilbert

My Free Gift to You!

As a way of saying thank you for downloading my book, I am willing to give you access to a selected group of readers who (every week or so) receive inspiring, life-changing kindle books at deep discounts, and sometimes even absolutely free.

Wouldn't it be great to get amazing Kindle offers delivered directly to your inbox?

Wouldn't it be great to be the first to know when I'm releasing new fresh and above all sharply discounted Relationship and Enlightenment content?

But why would I so something like this?

Why would I offer my books at such a low price and even give them away for free when they took me countless hours to produce?

Simple Because I want to spread the word.

For a few short days Amazon allows Kindle authors to promote their newly released books by offering them deeply discounted (up to 70% price discounts and even for free. This allows us to spread the word extremely quickly allowing users to download thousands and thousands of copies in a very short period of time.Once the timeframe has passed, these books will revert back to their normal selling price.

Thar's precisely why you will benefit from being the first to know when they can be downloaded for

So are you ready to claim your weekly Kindle books?

You are just one click away! Follow the link below and sign up to start receiving awesome content.

Thank you and Enjoy!

Table of contents

Introduction

I want to thank you and congratulate you for downloading the book, *The Mind of a Sociopath*

This book contains proven steps and strategies on how to identify and deal with sociopaths.

Do you have a person in your life that is just a little off and by a little off; I mean that they're full blown strange? Are they living like an emperor in their world and using everyone around them like pawns? Are they quite possibly the smartest person you know but not living a life that is actually fulfilling by normal standards? Are they nice to you, but only when they really want something form you?

You may have found yourself a sociopath. If that's the case, then this book is where you need to start looking to find the answers of how to identify a sociopath and what you can do to deal with one. It all starts right here, right now, and you're in the right place to get them out of your life.

Thanks again for downloading this book, I hope you enjoy it!

Wasn't Sherlock Supposed to be Cool?

Okay, so once upon a time, you might have watched *Sherlock* and thought that Sherlock Holmes was a pretty cool guy. He was so smart and so observant and so super funny. But, when you sit down and think about it, he probably would have been a super pain in the butt to work with. I mean, didn't he belittle Watson all the time and pretty much ruin any relationship he had at least once? Did he also have a cocaine addiction, or whatever snuff is, in the book? Also, didn't he like belittle everyone who wasn't him? Wait, wasn't Sherlock supposed to be cool? What the heck just happened? Have you and I been living a lie all this time?

No, you've just been a victim of a sociopath.

Stay calm, don't be alarmed, and whatever you do, don't scream. There's like a zillion sociopaths in movies and on television that you're probably guilty of taking extreme pleasure in but didn't notice what they truly were. They're snakes in the grass and that's a pretty common factor among all sociopaths. You usually don't notice what they are until it's pointed out to you, or you start putting the pieces together.

Sociopaths are all over society. They blend in and they are incredibly hard to spot unless they're already in your life, working their dark magic on you. I'm not going to say that sociopaths are evil, even though they're pretty darn close, but they're definitely not the kind of people that are in your life to be a helping hand to you.

In fact, unless you know how to spot a sociopath, there's a very good chance that you're going to fall prey to one in your life. Maybe you already have. There are a lot of people that end up dating a sociopath and start suspecting things are off less than a week into the relationship. So if you're in the situation where you think that you might have been caught in the web of a sociopath, then I'm going to show you just why you shouldn't think that Sherlock is a super cool guy and worthy of your time. In fact, I'm going to show you how to get a sociopath out of your life for good if you want them gone. It's all up to you what you want to do with them.

But the remaining truth that we all have to confront is that the odds of us running into a sociopath are pretty high right now and that doesn't seem to be going anywhere. So, if you're afraid that your boss, your parent, or maybe a close friend has definitely walked on the dark side and is among the hidden sociopath population, then maybe this is the book for you. Heck, maybe you're just interested in sociopaths. Well, that's a great reason to be here to. The point is: kick off your shoes and prepared to be mesmerized by the shocking, lurid, and downright complicated world of the common sociopath.

You're guaranteed to be intrigued.

Explain Yourself!

So, what is a sociopath? Well, a sociopath is a person with a deceptive personality disorder that reveals itself in a form of antisocial behavior and attitude that usually comes off across as a lack of conscience, morals, or care for others around them. That's great, but what does that really mean? Well, it means that we're going to have to start at the beginning of what they are on a completely social level.

Sociopaths have values. Like everyone else in the world, except for psychopaths, a sociopath has a value structure or an object of value that they define the rest of their lives and existence off of. However, this value system is skewed from what we would call normal in society. This manifests itself in an egocentric ideal that they hold themselves to and see the rest of the world as inferior to. It's a strange form of narcissism but not in the way that we would usually expect. But, whatever value system a sociopath has, it is skewed and isn't normal.

They don't hold value on others, because the rest of society is not calibrated into their moral compass. Since society or people in general are not important to the sociopath, their moral compass is built around something else. Because they have no value for people or those around them, a sociopath will most likely be seen as reclusive to avoid society, which turns out to be a problem to them or just a bother. Or worse, a sociopath will build a persona that is seen as charismatic, charming, and of great interest to society so that they can use them to further their agenda.

In a later chapter, we'll discuss the manifestations of sociopaths in society and we'll bring up how so many sociopaths actually reveal themselves in business industry with alarming numbers. Sociopaths usually fall into these two categories, but what remains consistent about both socially masked sociopaths and their reclusive brothers and sisters, is the fact that both are extremely driven to accomplish their goals.

Let's break it down a little more to understand what we mean by that. Sociopaths have values that do not exist like our own. The amygdala is the part of your brain that processes and exudes certain emotions: love, fear, anger, and sexual desire. Sociopaths have trouble in this region of the brain, which translates to a complete lack of certain emotions or just a whisper of what we all perceive as a yell of anger or love. With emotion out of the questions, a sociopath tends to develop goals much like you and I, but approaches them with a pragmatic and manipulative approach with their prime desire being that they achieve this goal. Without feelings like remorse, compassion, understanding, or tolerance, a sociopath essentially goes on the warpath to accomplish this goal. Once the goal is achieved, another goal is developed and they charge off after it. Think of them as an emotionless Jason Voorhees with a five year plan.

Granted, sociopaths are not violent by nature. If the person you're thinking of is violent, then you have a completely different beast to tackle there.

With only goals and desires that exist beyond the sexual, sociopaths are extremely intellectual. This means that they're smart. Knowledge is really just an acquisition game for them. Think of all that you could have learned in your life if you didn't have those darned, pesky emotions getting in the way. So, since they're smart and emotionless, sociopaths usually begin to realize that they're different and are both bitter and reclusive about this, or they seek to find a way to rectify the problem. After all, a lot of their goals depend upon having the understanding or support of people. In this sense, people become pawns in their game of accomplishing their goals. So, sociopaths tend to build false personas that are charming, charismatic, funny, and appealing to draw in people and manipulating them into getting what they need form them.

This is extremely unethical, but ethics are a thing for people who have remorse and compassion. So they don't care.

So how exactly are sociopaths dangerous to people? Well, very rarely are sociopaths physically dangerous to those around them. Like I said earlier, if you feel physically threatened by a sociopath, they're probably not a sociopath. But, sociopaths do have a form of danger that manifests itself in a completely different way. It's in the form of emotional and social damage.

For a sociopath, the people they interact with are nothing more to them than pawns or objectives in accomplishing their goals. Your desires, you interests, your feelings, and your career/dating life/financial situation are all expendable if it means that they're going to get to their objective faster.

When approaching a normal person, you are engaging in an intricate dance of emotions, information, and nonverbal communication that extends on multiple levels. Everything that you say to them or do around them is being processed in a normal, healthy standard to make their life better or to help them. Essentially, you're worried about being pleasant, sociable, kind, and polite.

A sociopath goes through something differently. If they approach you or you approach them, the situation is always the same. They begin sizing you up, studying you and analyzing whether you are valuable to them or not. A sociopath will usually stick around in a conversation until this is determined. If you're found to be wanting or not at all useful to them, they're most likely going to kick you to the curb and move on to something more appropriate for their needs. Sorry, better luck next time. Their questions might be subtle if they're a social sociopath, or they might be direct if they don't have an interest to play the game they consider life to be. Once it's determined, however, that you're useful to them. That's when they begin to shift g ears. For a sociopath that has developed the necessary social veneer, they will immediately begin to shift gears. They will start to try and read you and figure out what it is you want, like, or are looking for. Remember, sociopaths have had their entire lives to observe and watch people to figure out what it is they want.

Once they've found what they need to manipulate you or use you to their own advantage, you're done for. I hope that you got a favor out of them first, because if they owe you a favor, they're never going to let you collect.

So, what is a sociopath? A sociopath is a person with a blockage, disruption, or issue with their amygdala which robs them of emotions and the ability to develop a value system based on the emotions that we all have. Instead, they become task oriented, driven, and valued. Without emotions, they become very smart and quickly develop a manipulative or disdainful outlook toward those around them to accomplish the goals and objectives that they have. Once a sociopath has deemed you as a possible accessory to their objective, they will utilize you in whatever fashion they can get, regardless of the damage that is inflicted or caused by you. Essentially, they will destroy your entire life if it means they can stand a little higher on the ruins of your life.

They're not that cool once you get to know them.

But, before we go any farther. We need to establish something.

Are you sure you're dealing with a sociopath?

Gordon Gecko or Jason Voorhees?

Until not too long ago, sociopaths were actually classified as people who were suffering from minor or lesser cases of psychopathy. Thankfully, recently, we've been able to determine that though the two share enormous and numerable similarities and disturbing qualities, they are actually distinctly different. Thankfully, if you're dealing with a sociopath, you got the better deal right now. If you determine, after reading this chapter, that you're actually dealing with a psychopath, then you're in some hot water.

So, I'm going to go over the definition of what a psychopath is and explain them in a little bit of detail and then explain why the differences are distinct and important. A psychopath is a person who has also developed a blockage, growth, or disturbance in theair amygdala which strips them completely void of having any kind of a value system. Not only are they emotionless, they don't even have a value on what they begin to perceive as a goal in their lives. Seeing that they're completely different from those around them and having no values to build an identity upon, a psychopath builds an elaborate lie, except they have nothing for it to stand upon. Once a psychopath has a false identity that they wear as a mask, they wander through society trying to blend in and act normal why they know all the time that they're different.

Feeling a void inside of them where values and emotions should be residing, psychopaths seek to fill this emptiness with something that will bring value to them. Since they are incapable of having a value system, this builds a vacuum that cannot be filled at all. They're left to wander, hunger, angry, and destroying anything that gets in their way or is used up. They're like vampires. This sounds eerily similar to the sociopath description, but there are a few differences that will make you breathe a sigh of relief when you find out that you're dealing with a sociopath rather than a psychopath.

The first difference is that sociopaths understand that violence has a social consequence that they are not capable of escaping. Since they have a value system that is skewed, a sociopath will come to understanding that getting convicted of murder or suspected of murder will probably leave them unable to fulfill their goals. It's much easier to manipulate them into destroying themselves, rather than actually killing them. So, if you have a sociopath in your life, very rarely will they kill you because you've left their life. In fact, they'll probably move on and find someone to replace the hole that you left in their plan.

The second difference is that a sociopath, if they want to be, can be brought to understanding that there is something wrong with them. It is hard, invasive, and requires years of dedication on the part of the sociopath, but they can be brought to understand that their moral compass is skewed. A psychopath has no value system, no emotions, and no desire to change that. At best, they are institutionalized and medicated to suppress their more violent natures and tendencies. If you are of extreme value to a sociopath, there is a very high chance that you can actually get them to realize that they need help. It can feel manipulative, because it will have to be, but in the end, you can get them the help that they truly need.

Finally, a sociopath's personality actually has some credibility to it. Our identities are built upon what it is we value. Our values tell us what we stand up for, what we care about, and what we're not willing to risk or lose, no matter what. Without a value system, we lack an entire identity. Psychopaths have no values and are incapable of forming genuine values to things, which means that their entire identity does not exist. You cannot reach something deep down inside of a vacuum, because there is only darkness and emptiness. Sociopaths have value, it's just skewed to not incorporate those around them. So, their personality, while they may be superficial and fake to those around them, actually has a core that can be penetrated. When dealing with a sociopath, you can find that there's something real and that there's something legitimate to them, regardless of the candy coating on the exterior that they have.

So, now that we've established a difference between psychopaths and sociopaths and realized that the words aren't just interchangeable for the convenience of the person talking; are you sure that you're dealing with a sociopath?

If you're dealing with a psychopath and they have fixated on you and have decided that you're of some importance to them, then you're in serious trouble. If you're dealing with someone with violent outbursts and psychopathic behavior, I would suggest doing more research to make sure that you're dealing with one. Paranoia might come into play here, but to be on the safe side, do your homework. Once you've established that they're a psychopath, it's time to get help. Call your biggest, baddest, toughest friend and talk to them. Get people you can trust to start setting up an escape route and plan for you and make sure that you start the legal work for a restraining order.

Then, once that's in place, get the heck out of Camp Crystal Lake.

Psychopaths cannot be reformed or changed, so don't think that there's something deep down inside there that you can change. You can't. This is serious, life threatening stuff. Make a clean break and get the heck out of there. Move into a house with bars on the windows and pray that they move on to something else.

But if you've got a sociopath, we've got a whole lot more to chat about.

The Checklist!

Okay, so we've officially answered the question that we all have rolling around in our mind: is the person I'm thinking of a sociopath, psychopath, or just a weirdo? Wait, no we haven't! All we know is what sociopaths are and why they're different from psychopaths. But how do we know if someone is actually a sociopath? I mean, what does that look like? Should we start avoiding and locking up everyone who smokes a pipe and solves crimes or works on Wall Street? If that's the case, we're going to need to take a better look at what a sociopath looks like in its natural habitat, aka all around you.

There's an estimated four percent of the population who is classified as sociopath and that means that they're pretty much everywhere. While the majority is declared as being male, women are yet again proven to be the more sane sex than men thanks to the power of statistics. So if there is four percent of the population among us that are sociopaths, then we're in some serious trouble, because one in twenty five is officially skewed.

So here's a list of the things that most sociopaths give away or have that indicates that there's something officially wrong with them. Some of them are subtle and some of them are glaringly obvious, but the majority of them are going to make you think of a few people. Remember, they need to have a fairly decent accumulation of this list to actually be classified as a sociopath. Please, do not be disappointed if your weird cousin who locks himself in the basement is not actually a sociopath and just unusual.

<u>Highly Intelligent</u>

Here is the most frightening and terrible fact about sociopaths that makes you want to bite your nails in terror and cry at the wasted potential. When a sociopath develops their value system and has something to focus their interest on, they begin to learn everything there is to know about the topic and they start to devour all they can to become the best at what they can learn. What this produces is a highly intelligent, highly efficient, and extremely ruthless asset to whatever field or market they decide to pursue.

They know that better school grades lead to greater college opportunities which will in turn lead them to an even better chance at becoming someone famous in their desired field. With this cutthroat and ruthless mentality of doing whatever it takes to accomplish their designs, they become dangerous members of whatever field they enter and make them someone you would rather be working with than against.

But, this doesn't always translate into success. Sometimes monetary wealth is not what they're interested. For example, some have an interest to simply accomplish their desired goal, not to have the excess wealth and fame that comes along with the act. However, a majority of the time, it does come with wealth, prestige, and popularity that they use to help further their goals.

No matter where you find them, your sociopath is going to know their stuff and they're going to be really well educated in whatever leads them to success in their desired field of interest. So, don't try to match them in a contest of wits.

Antisocial

This is the key indicator that most sociopaths are actually sociopaths, but it's actually one of the hardest indicators to truly spot because of one of the other indicators that we'll address later. Most sociopaths who have developed a value that exists out in the real world find a need for human contact, but some never develop this need. In fact, they gather the supplies they need and simply disappear from society altogether, only coming out when they truly need to.

For those that have developed the veneer of social behaviors, they're harder to distinguish, but you can begin to read their movements quite well. For example: do they only come out to social events when they have a clear objective for being there? Are they there to meet a certain individual? Do they want to gain notoriety for what they're doing? Is there something they seek to gain form being at a social event other than hanging out with people and leisurely networking? If they always have an objective for being somewhere, it's a pretty good indicator that they're a sociopath.

Remember that a sociopath is always objective oriented and won't bother wasting time with others if they don't need them for something. They're going to be too busy furthering their objective instead of going to some stupid party because of some stupid person's stupid birthday. They're above that. Which brings us to indicator number two.

Superiority

Does this person have a distinct belief that they are above others? This will most often manifest itself with delusions of grandeur. This might be justified or it might not be, the point is that they see it that way and they cannot fathom why you or others cannot actually see how great they are. A lot of times, this isn't completely unwarranted, because like we've discussed earlier, they're usually brilliant.

Their superiority also will never fail to show itself. When a sociopath is in their element and someone is seeking to climb the latter that they don't deem worthy of doing so, a sociopath will make an example of these upstarts. Demonstrating their superiority and making themselves seen as better is all done in another day's work for a sociopath. In the end, they see themselves as better and regard all others as inferior to their might and power. All hail the great and glorious sociopath.

Remorseless

Your failure and destruction means nothing to a sociopath, because you are nothing more than a pawn on the board. The sick thing is that they don't even see themselves as kings, but rather as the person playing chess. That's right, they've donned a god-like role in their own game. So when they approach situations, their stance is a winner-takes-all mode that will leave any action, no matter how devastating to those left in the bloody wake, as justifiable. This is a dangerous approach to take to anyone or anything in life, but a sociopath sees this as more than acceptable, so long as it means that they accomplish their goals or just get a little closer. This sense of remorselessness will often manifest itself in smaller decisions, rather than just in their larger decisions. Leaving you at home because you're going to make them late is a perfectly acceptable decision to a sociopath who has places to be and people to see. Has the person you're thinking about taken a special interest in being ruthless or cutthroat? Do they get people fired, into trouble, or into compromising situations to further their own agenda?

A Lack of Empathy

Sometimes things really hurt in life, regardless of what role we played in them coming around. For example, when your boyfriend or girlfriend dumps you for not being the right one. Well, maybe the fact that this break up doesn't affect your friends directly, it still hurts them to see their dear friend hurting so much. As for your sociopath, what do they freaking care? Is your love life in any way, shape, or form relevant to them conquering the world of their goal? No, then get the heck out of their way! That's not a normal trait or behavior, but you will see this over and over again. In fact, you might see something far more disturbing or worse. You might see a social sociopath trying to act like they feel bad for you. It's about as natural as seeing a Terminator petting a dog.

Their lack of empathy is one of their more noticeable traits and will really manifest itself in movies. Over analyzing, coldly calculating, and deliberately failing to see the emotional sides of stories or events will mark them as a sociopath before you begin to suspect anything else. This might actually be the first indicator that flared your attention that there is something wrong with them. This coldhearted nature isn't their fault, but it certainly makes them awkward and it points them out as being different. However, it could be hard to spot, because of the next indicator.

Sublimely Charming

Social sociopaths who know how to get what they want know exactly what they need to do to make people think that they're normal and that they like them. Heck, they will sell a snowman more snow if that means they're closer to their goal. Sociopaths know that they are different from society or they don't have what it takes to be normal, but they've got the next best thing. They've got a mind that can analyze, calculate, and establish a false identity that will work with charm, seduction, finesse, and extreme desire to all around them. It's practically a game to them.

By answering questions in a negative light, you're telling them exactly what they need to say to get you to like them. Not only that, you're probably giving up information as to whether they need you in their lives and in their goals or not. It's a slippery slope, but if you're involved with a sociopath, it's probably a good chance that they're extremely charming and drew you in like a moth to the flame. That's extremely easy to understand because the next point is going to be a doozey that you probably picked up on in a heartbeat too now.

They're Liars

Sociopaths are all liars and that means that they're easy to entrap in their own lies. They have lots of reasons to lie and we're going to go into a major one in the next point, but right now, let's focus on the things they lie about. One of the easiest ways to pick out if they're a liar is to analyze what you know about them. If a sociopath builds a false persona around your answers to their questions and then they calibrate their personality accordingly, then they probably don't care about half the stuff they pretended to like or know anything about.

For example, if a sociopath needs you and through the course of your introduction, you revealed that you have an extreme love of zydeco music and they also expressed an interest in it. Test them on it. Ask them who their favorite washboard player is. You're going to find that their superficial lies that they built to make you think that you're kindred spirits is actually a glass house of cards just waiting to be blown down. Pick your analogy, but it won't be hard to figure out. That's the point.

The funny thing is, they probably won't even bat an eyelash that you found out.

Manipulation

Another reason why sociopaths are so keen on lying is that they're manipulating those around them all the time. Even people that they might profess to have an attraction to is just a pawn in their grand game. Sociopaths are known to spread rumors and lies around offices and institutes to start fires and spark rivalries that will open the door for them to move forward and advance in their main objective. If you're involved in their life somehow right now, that probably means that you're being manipulated or that you're going to be manipulated. No one can be allowed to rise above them, beat them, or destroy them.

The ironic thing about this is that when it comes to dealing with sociopaths, manipulating them becomes one of the easiest ways of getting rid of them. When someone else starts playing their one-man-game, things get thrown off fast.

Egocentric

Finally and without any surprise really, sociopaths are notoriously egocentric. Everything is about them. Everything is about their ambitions and their goals. If you get in their way, then you have to be removed from the game or the equation. They don't like having to deal with you and their other problems at the same time. It's all about them and if you're in their life, it's only because you're helping them or opening a door for them. That's all. You're a glorified doorknob.

The Hunter Becomes the Hunted

So you've got a bona fide sociopath on your hands and you know what they are without a shadow of a doubt crossing your mind. That's good. You're leagues ahead of most people and that means that you've identified a major problem in your romantic or career life. This isn't going to be a problem for long, because it's time to start dealing with trouble maker and if you can't, maybe you can get them some help along the way or stop them from hurting anyone else around you.

First thing you've got to do is keep on doing what you're already doing. Educating yourself is vitally important. There are a lot of resources out there and you've got to start treating this thing like it's a conspiracy theory. Don't go shouting it down at the town square with a bell that you've decided to ring. That's going to bring speculation and set them to work targeting you for termination.

Don't become a target. That's number two. It's time to start playing things smart. The thing about sociopaths is that they probably already know your weaknesses and know exactly what they need to do to take you out of the equation if you become a target. So make sure that everything is normal and that you start working in discretion.

The next thing you've got to start doing to make sure that they don't manipulate, lie, or use you is to start thinking like a sociopath. Expect whatever they say to you is a lie or that they're trying to get you to do something to help further their goals. If they relay a message, double-check the person who supposedly sent it. Don't waste a chance to find out if they're manipulating you and log it. Keep a secret record of everything that they do and don't let them ever find it. When it comes to things that you have to say to them, be cold and calculating. Don't give them any information they don't need and certainly don't let them get you to do things for them. In fact, try making them do things for you instead.

Finally, when you have enough information to get rid of them or to file a restraining order. It's time to go to your boss or the police. If you're dating them, now is the time to enact the emergency escape plan that you should have been plotting with your friends. Get out of dodge, file a restraining order, and remove yourself form their life entirely. Don't worry about their feelings, because they won't give a single tear about yours. If you're in a professional environment, gather any conspirators that you have with you and approach their superior. Reveal whatever unethical practices that they've been doing and walk away. That's in their hands. If you get them fired or if you get them in trouble, be ready for the consequences.

After you've dealt with them and made a clean break, the only time you should ever come in contact with them again is to advise them that they need to seek professional help and if they approach you again that you will call the police.

Let me make something clear to you: you're not going to be able to reform them. In fact, you'll be lucky if a professional will even be able to get through to them. Sociopaths are notoriously ignorant and spiteful toward those that get in their way. No matter how much you like them or think that you love them, you've got to accept that you're in love with a lie. Yes, there's something to them deep down inside, but that's not going to be something that you and the power of love will be able to get to.

The only time you should ever give a sociopath a second chance in a relationship is if there is documented and verified proof that they have sought out help and that they have taken the necessary steps to become someone that they have never truly been. This is a difficult and it's a terrifying path for them to walk, but if they actually receive the help, there is a chance that they might become a really decent and wonderful person.

It requires a complete transformation and adjustment of what they are and what they know. With years of therapy and help by professionals, they can turn their life around, but you are not that person. Seek out a professional before you depart from their life and see if they can't get them help, but that's the extent of what you should ever do for them. After all, they were looking to use you and leave you for nothing when they were done. So don't have any pity or remorse for them. They are ruthless, calculating, and heartless people that destroy lives. If they get the help they need, then you can pity them.

But not a second before.

Watson Moved on with His Life

Sociopaths are self-destructive people by nature and they are on a collision course with the reality of the world that they've built around them. They will derive some sort of satisfaction from the world that they've built, but it will taste sour and hollow to them. That's why so many sociopaths continue to keep working, keep striving, and keep building even after their goals are accomplished. They know that they're missing what it is that makes humans so satisfied and so content. It's the heart of humanity that they're lacking and like machines working on a task, they need a new goal to keep moving.

All jokes and silly analogies aside, sociopaths are people too and there are a lot of them out in the world. Many of them have flooded to the professional careers that we hold in high esteem and have a lot of power to make the decisions that affect the world around them. They have a lot of power and a lot of authority and it's scary to think that they're in charge, but that doesn't mean that they have to always be like that.

Sociopaths can be reformed and they can be taught to adjust their moral compass. The great thing is that unlike psychopaths, they actually have a moral compass and they can be shown the errors of their ways. By a little compassion and a little love, we can do everything we can to bring their lives around, but at a distance. There are professionals who will be more than willing to get their hands dirty and start changing things around in their lives. They know how to make them see the errors of their ways.

But for those of you out there that are dealing with them in the professional world, just avoid them. They'll find someone else who will help them achieve their goals and they rarely have patience for underlings if they rise above you. Most of the time, they won't even care that you exist unless they need something shifted below them. It's their equals and those above them that have to worry about them. Of course, they'll probably be the person that fires you, but that's an unfortunate symptom. If they become your boss, just do the best work you can and start networking for a job elsewhere.

Just leave that sociopath in their own world and move on.

After all, Watson did in the end.

Conclusion

Before you go, I'd like to say thank you for purchasing my book.

I know you could have picked so many other books to read on understanding Sociopaths. But you took a chance on me.

So A Big thanks for downloading this book and reading it all the way to completion.

Now I would like to ask a _small_ favor.

Could you please take a minute or two to leave a review for this book on Amazon?

Click here

The feedback will help me continue to publish more kindle books that will help people to get better results in their lives.

And if you found it helpful in anyway then please let me know :-)

Preview of My New Book..

Help! I'm In Love With A Narcissist

So There's This Person...

So you've met this person who seems to have it all together, it all figured out, and the cat's in the bag. They're the kind of person who steps into the room with the presence of a floodlight and when they leave, it feels like they took the oxygen with them. They're captivated by all the boring stuff you've crammed into your calendars and call a life, but more importantly, they make you feel great. Every word you say is scooped up and filed away in their brains because they're actively engaging with you. They're making you feel like you're the only person in the room.

I mean, they're dedicated to themselves. They've been grooming themselves impeccably, or maybe they've moved beyond that. Maybe they've transcended the need to look good and they're just all about their intellectual prowess that they're willing to share with you—YOU, mere mortal! This person is the one person you know that could sell snow to an Inuit.

Sure, they might talk like they're trying to sell you something, or you might get the chills when you shake their hand, but come on, they're really great! They're a riot to be around and there's no way that you're just going to give up on hanging out with someone this cool.

But after a while, it might grate against you. After all, you watch as they move from one person to the next at parties, dancing around like the social butterfly that they are. It might start out as jealousy that you're not getting the majority of their time. It might bother you that all that special treatment that they gave you is just their average operating mode, which they treat everyone incredible, regardless of whom they are or what their lives are like. But after a moment, the jealousy is going to fade, because there's a truth hiding in there that is just nagging at you—clawing at you—to get out.

This might be because you're picking up on something no quite right about them. It means that you might be picking up on a subtle reality that's lurking behind those charming eyes and that million dollar smile that's starting to rub you the wrong way more and more. It's something more and most likely, you're picking up on the fact that the person you're bothered by might be a narcissist.

Of course, there are Narcissists and there are narcissists. A subtle difference in writing that makes all the difference and we're going to talk about both of them in this book. There are people out there that are really full of themselves. They're people who make life difficult for themselves and for those that are working with them and there are ways for us as regular people to deal with them. There are ways around them and there are ways to truly identify them.

After all, you don't want to peg Cool Jim as a Narcissist when he just has an over inflated ego. So where do you start? Well, reading this book was a great decision, because we're going to figure out together if Cool Jim is really someone you should be avoiding or if this is someone that you should just try your hardest to ignore and maybe just avoid at parties. In the end, we're going to find out what it is that you're dealing with.

So, want to go hunting for a narcissist? Or is it a Narcissist?

O Muses

So, once upon a time, the Greeks decided that there was a story that needed to be told. It was the tale of how a river god and a nymph decided to get together for a little tryst that resulted in the birth of an exceptionally beautiful young man you was declared as Narcissus. Now, this wasn't a man who was just 90's Brad Pitt gorgeous, but the male version of Helen of Troy. He drove the ladies and the men crazy. People wanted him and they wanted to be him. There's something about this guy that really made people go wild. They wanted him and when you're a hot commodity, demand tends to turn to worship and worship does something nasty for the people who aren't ready for it.

Narcissus had a commodity that was in high demand. That means that people were all over him and the desire for him is what inevitably drove Narcissus to a dark, cold place that made him resentful and spiteful of those that loved and desired him. As they flocked to him, Narcissus became a tool and a douche. He was rude and mean and cruel to everyone that came after him. In essence, he came to believe exactly what they told him he was a little too much.

Seeing this, the goddess of revenge decided that it was time to bring him down to reality after his cruelty and rudeness toward others. So while Narcissus was out hunting all manly and such, he came across an enchanted pool that the goddess of revenge made just for him. Well, when Narcissus found the pool, he gazed into it and found his reflection and fell in love with it. For the first time in his life, Narcissus found in love with someone, only that it's himself. Gazing into the pool, night and day passed as he gazed at the reflection in the pool.

Then, before anyone can tell him what an idiot he's being, his selfish love is rewarded with him falling into the pool and drowning because he couldn't take his eyes off himself.

There's a lot that can be taken away from this story and there's a lot that is freakishly familiar with what's going to follow in these next few chapters. So there's this happy little moment at the end of this chapter that I get to tell you why this story is important and it's going to be great. So here you go:

Click Here To Read The Rest Of

Help! I'm In Love With A Narcissist

P.S. You'll find many more books like this and others under my name Michele Gilbert.

Don't miss them… here is a short list.

Wicca: The Ultimate Beginners Guide For Witches and Warlocks: Learn Wicca Magic

The Introvert's Advantage: The Introverts Guide To Succeeding In An Extrovert World

Stop Playing Mind Games: How To Free Yourself Of Controlling And Manipulating Relationships

Instant Charisma: A Quick And Easy Guide To Talk, Impress, And Make Anyone Like You

Chakras: Understanding The 7 Main Chakras For Beginners: The Ultimate Guide To Chakra Mindfulness, Balance and Healing

Practicing Mindfulness: Living in the moment through Meditation: Everyday Habits and Rituals to help you achieve inner peace

Adrenal Fatigue: What Is Adrenal Fatigue Syndrome And How To Reset Your Diet And Your Life

Sleep Tight: Overcome Insomnia and Sleep Disorders for a better more restful sleep!

Stop Back Pain Now!: Back Pain Remedies and Treatments so you can live a pain free life!

The Arthritis Pain Cure: How to find Arthritis Pain Relief and live a happy pain free life!

The Headache Pain Cure: How to find Headache Pain Relief and live a happy Pain Free Life!

Stop Panic Attacks and Anxiety Disorders without Drugs Now!: Overcome Panic, Stress and Anxiety and live a happy pain free life!

The Breakup Recovery Guide: Advice for Surviving Heartbreak, Letting Go and Thriving in an exciting new life!

The Friendship Guide to Finding Friends Forever: How to Find, Make and Keep Quality Friendships After your Breakup

The Credit Fix: Leave behind credit card debt and poor credit scores and get your life back!

How To Stop Being Jealous And Insecure: Overcome Insecurity And Relationship Jealousy

So I Am Dating A Psycopath: Now What?

Michele Gilbert was born and raised in Brooklyn, New York. Drawn to literature and writing at a young age, she enrolled at Brooklyn College and majored in English. After graduation Michele did not begin writing immediately, instead she embarked on a career in the finance industry and spent the next thirty years on Wall Street.

Serendipity struck when she least expected it. After ending a long-term relationship, Michele found herself lost and unsure what the future held. She began to read books on grief and loss, looking for answers. Those led her to delve deeper into the Law of Attraction and its power. What resulted was remarkable. Not only had she begun to heal, she had also rekindled her former love of writing and discovered her life's purpose.

The years have taken her through many twists and turns, but she learned valuable lessons along the way. Today she publishes books-mostly self-help and metaphysical in nature-and feels compelled to share her knowledge with those facing similar experiences. Her greatest hope is to inspire others and show them ways to overcome adversity and gracefully accept life's inevitable low points.

Going forward, she plans to incorporate more teachings of self-help, finance and meditation. Regular meditation is very beneficial to her progress as she forges a new life. Morning rituals and positive incantations are other practices Michele embraces; they are very restorative in daily life.

As an avid hiker, Michele and fellow club members often hike the picturesque Jersey Pine Barrens. She is a history buff, voracious reader, baseball fanatic and a foodie. She also proudly supports Trout Unlimited-a national non-profit organization dedicated to conserving, protecting and restoring North America's Coldwater fisheries and their watersheds.

Michele currently resides forty minutes from Atlantic City and the Jersey Shore. She makes her home with a Blue Russian rescue cat named Jersey, though she isn't exactly sure who rescued who.

Michele really enjoys publishing books that can make a difference in people's lives. If you have any suggestions or would like to have a specific topic covered in a future book, please send an email to michelegilbertbooks@gmail.com and we will get back to you.

Thanks for reading!

www.ingramcontent.com/pod-product-compliance
Lightning Source LLC
Chambersburg PA
CBHW050928290526
45792CB00002B/934